High-Interest/Low-Readability Nonfiction

Fascinating Machines

by Kathryn Wheeler

Carson-Dellosa Publishing Company, Inc.
Greensboro, North Carolina

Credits

Editor:
Ashley Anderson

Layout Design:
Van Harris

Inside Illustrations:
Donald O'Connor

Cover Design:
Annette Hollister-Papp
Peggy Jackson

Cover Illustration:
Tara Tavonatti

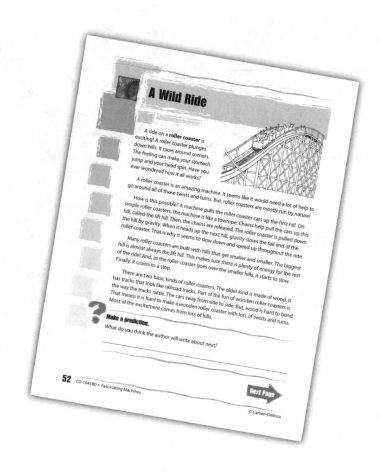

ISBN 1-59441-316-9

Table of Contents

Introduction... 4

Not So Simple 5

Once Upon a Time... 7

The Sky Is the Limit 9

Racing through Space 11

Where in the World Are You? 13

Extreme Life-Saving Machines.. 15

Ice Monsters.. 17

Quack, Quack!.. 19

Faster Than a Speeding Bullet 21

Sweet Machines 23

Touch the Vote 25

Fly Me to the Moon 27

Flying and Spying 29

The Machines That Found *Titanic*................................... 31

A World of Robots 34

A New Vision 37

Inside a Computer 40

Mars or Bust 43

What Is a Hybrid? 46

Cars of the Future... 49

A Wild Ride.. 52

At Home in Space.. 55

The Most Fascinating Machine 59

Answer Key.. 63

Introduction

Struggling readers in the upper-elementary and middle grades face a difficult challenge. While many of their peers are reading fluently, they are still working to acquire vocabulary and comprehension skills. They face a labyrinth of standardized tests, which can be a nightmare for struggling readers. And, they face another major difficulty—the challenge of remaining engaged and interested while working to improve reading skills.

High-Interest/Low-Readability Nonfiction: Fascinating Machines can help! All of the articles in this book are written at a fourth-grade reading level with an interest level from grade 4 to adult.

Throughout the book, the stories use repeated vocabulary to help students acquire and practice new words. The stories are crafted to grab students' attention while honing specific reading skills, such as uncovering author's purpose; defining vocabulary; making predictions; and identifying details, synonyms, antonyms, and figures of speech. Most of the comprehension questions parallel standardized-test formats so that students can become familiar with the structure without the pressure of a testing situation. And, the articles even utilize the familiar "Next Page" arrows and "Stop" signs seen in most standardized tests. The questions also include short-answer formats for writing practice.

Best of all, this book will build confidence in students as they learn that reading is fun, enjoyable, and fascinating!

Note: Stories that include measurements, such as a distance or weight, also feature a convenient conversion box with measurements rounded to the nearest hundredth. Students will find this useful as they become familiar with converting standard and metric measurements. If students are not currently studying measurement conversion, simply instruct them to ignore the box. Or, cover it when making copies of a story.

Not So Simple

Do you think that all machines are really complicated? Stop and think again! Every machine in the world is made of **simple machines**. Simple machines are all around us. We could not live our lives without them.

One kind of simple machine is the **wedge**. A wedge drives into something and divides it. An ax is a wedge. So is a fork! A boat is made so that the *bow*, or front, is a wedge. It slices through the water.

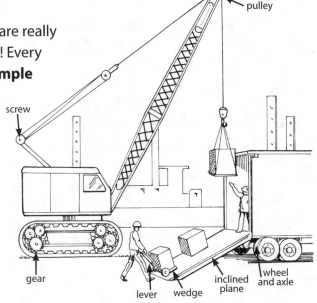

Another kind of simple machine is the **gear**. Think about a clock. The gears inside a clock turn. They change the energy of the motor into movement. The hands of the clock can move because of this change.

Then, there is the **inclined plane**. This simple machine slants so that things roll or move down it. The bottom of a bathtub is an inclined plane. It moves the water to the drain. The blades of a fan are inclined planes, too. The slanted blades push air to make a breeze.

An important simple machine is actually a pair: the **wheel and axle**. The wheel turns on the axle. This helps things move. Cars, trucks, and trains all use this simple machine. We even use it to open doors. A doorknob is also a wheel and axle. It turns so that the latch of the door can move.

There are other simple machines, too. A **pulley** helps people raise and lower window blinds. It can raise and lower a flag on a flagpole. It also helps rock climbers stay safe. A **lever** is found in the handles of scissors and the switches of lights. A **screw** doesn't only work with wood. It also helps people put lids on jars. It helps people put lightbulbs into sockets. Simple machines are fascinating because they are everywhere!

Next Page

Not So Simple

Answer the questions below.

1. An example of a pulley is—
   a. a drain in a sink.
   b. on a flagpole.
   c. a metal attachment that connects a climber to a safety rope.
   d. b. and c.

2. Read the following sentence from the story and answer the question.

   It turns so that the latch of the door can move.

   What is a *latch*?
   a. It is the part of the door that holds it closed.
   b. It is the part of the door that lets it swing open and shut.
   c. It is the part of the door that fits into the frame.
   d. none of the above

3. Circle three words or phrases that tell about the wedge.

   ax   splits things apart

   uses gears   uses wheels

   flagpole   drives into something

4. What is the *bow* of a boat?
   a. the front
   b. the back
   c. the sails
   d. the motor

5. A gear turns to change _____

   into _____ , like

   the gears of a _____

   move the hands.

6. Which of the following is one feature of simple machines?
   a. They are everywhere.
   b. They are used in every machine on Earth.
   c. They make our modern lives possible.
   d. all of the above

7. Think about the objects around you. What is an example of a simple machine that is not mentioned in the story? Write your answer in a complete sentence.

   _____

   _____

   _____

   _____

   _____

   _____

   STOP

Once Upon a Time

Is every machine on the cutting edge? Maybe! When something is first made, it is a *breakthrough*. That means no one ever thought of it before. It changes the way people live. But, these amazing machines of the past don't stay on the cutting edge. New inventions take over.

The **abacus**, a counting board with beads on it, changed everything. Before it was invented, people counted on their fingers. They had to keep track of numbers in their heads. The abacus may have been invented in China. It did not come to Europe until about 1000 A.D. when traders brought it to Italy. People were afraid of the strange invention. Were people meant to count so high?

Another big breakthrough was the **printing press**. Before 1450, books were rare. If you wanted a book, you had to wait a long time! All books were written by hand. Sometimes, it took years to make just one book. Then, a man named Johannes Gutenberg figured out how to make *type*, or wooden blocks with letters carved on them. He fitted them into a frame. The machine pressed the inked type against paper. In 1452, he made 200 books. People were amazed. Today, people can print thousands of books at one time. Computers help them make text changes and run printing machines.

Computers are the extreme machines of our time. There are still people who can remember a time before there were computers. Now, computers are everywhere. They are part of our everyday lives. They help run cars. They keep track of records. They fly planes and cook food! Someday, people will look back. They will think our computers seem old-fashioned. Like the abacus and the printing press, one day computers will no longer seem extreme.

Once Upon a Time

Answer the questions below.

1. What kind of *type* is talked about in the story?

   a. movements on a keyboard to make letters
   b. wooden blocks that have letters carved on them
   c. different groups of people or animals
   d. none of the above

2. Read the following sentence from the story and answer the question.

   But, these amazing machines of the past don't stay on the cutting edge.

   What is another way to say *stay on the cutting edge* in this sentence?

   a. stay the most important breakthrough
   b. sit on the edge of the knife
   c. go back to the edge of the past
   d. none of the above

3. Which of the following sentences is the BEST summary of the story?

   a. Many things seem to be on the cutting edge when they are invented, but they aren't.
   b. Many things are breakthroughs at the time they are invented, but then they become part of everyday life.
   c. Amazing machines were invented long ago but not now.
   d. The abacus was a big breakthrough in math.

4. What is an *abacus*? Write your answer in a complete sentence.

   _____

   _____

5. Why did the printing press change life so much?

   a. Before the printing press, it took a long time to make a book.
   b. Because of the printing press, books could be made much faster.
   c. Before type was invented, books had to be written by hand.
   d. all of the above

6. Think about new machines that have been invented in your lifetime. Name one that is "on the cutting edge" in your opinion. Why do you think so? Write your answer in complete sentences.

   _____

   _____

   _____

   _____

   _____

The Sky Is the Limit

Throughout time, people have wanted to build big buildings. Think about the pyramids in Egypt. Think about the huge churches in Europe. Until the 1880s, most buildings were not very tall. In the past, people thought a 10-story building was high. Why? Because a building's walls had to be very thick at the bottom to support all of that weight on top.

By the end of the 1800s, tall buildings called **skyscrapers** were everywhere. What changed? A big breakthrough in making steel changed things. Suddenly, there were machines that could make long steel beams, or *girders*. These steel beams were much stronger than iron. How are they used? First, tall steel columns are locked into the building's base. Next, the columns are connected by the girders. This forms the building's skeleton. It supports the weight of the building. The walls do not have to be thick. They can be made of thin panels and windows. This thin outside layer is called the *curtain wall*.

The really amazing thing about skyscrapers is that these huge buildings are built using simple machines! Giant cranes lift the steel beams to the tops of the buildings. Cranes are made of two simple machines: pulleys and the wheel and axle. Wedges are used to help cut the panels for the curtain walls. Large screws called *bolts* are used to help hold the pieces in place. Other machines, like those used to weld beams together, have gears inside to make their motors work.

Once the skyscrapers are built, people need to get to the top floors. Simple machines help then, too. Stairs—a type of inclined plane—have been used for many years. But, walking up 100 floors takes a long time and is very hard work! So, people use the elevator, which uses a pulley.

Next Page

Name_____ Date_____

The Sky Is the Limit

Answer the questions below.

1. Read the following sentence from the story and answer the question.

   A big breakthrough in making steel changed things.

   What is a *breakthrough*?
   a. a sudden understanding of how to do something new
   b. a breaking of a solid object
   c. a ground breaking for a new building
   d. a grid used to hold something up

2. Which two simple machines make a crane? Write your answer in a complete sentence.

   _____

   _____

3.–6. Write T for true and F for false.

3. _____ Until the 1980s, people could only build buildings about 10 stories high.

4. _____ Wedges are used to cut panels for walls.

5. _____ Elevators use an inclined plane.

6. _____ The columns and girders of a skyscraper connect together.

7. Which of the following is NOT a feature of a skyscraper?
   a. interlocking parts that hold the weight evenly
   b. tall steel columns
   c. girders that connect the columns
   d. a heavy base that is wider than the rest of the building

8. Choose the word that BEST completes the following sentence:

   The wall of glass and thin panels on a skyscraper is called the _____ .
   a. girder
   b. window wall
   c. column
   d. curtain wall

9. Do you think skyscrapers are fascinating? Why or why not? Write your answer in complete sentences.

   _____

   _____

   _____

   _____

   _____

STOP

Racing through Space

Satellites were once very secret spy machines. Now, we use them for all kinds of help on Earth. A satellite is almost like a radio in space. It moves around our planet. It sends signals back to us.

How do satellites get to space? One way is to send them in a rocket. People can also send a satellite for a ride on a space shuttle. The satellite rides in the shuttle's *cargo bay*, the place where supplies are stored. When the shuttle gets to the right place, it lets the satellite go into space.

Once the satellite is in space, it has a job to do. Satellites help us in many ways. Some of them watch the weather. A weather satellite carries cameras. It takes pictures of Earth. It shows the pattern of clouds and storms. Other satellites help with telephone, radio, and TV signals. The signals bounce off the satellite. Then, they go back to a certain place on Earth. Another kind of satellite helps save lives. It finds ships and planes that are in trouble.

Satellites are used for secret work, too. Satellites take pictures of other countries. They help watch troops and equipment as they are moved. Most people do not know very much about these spy satellites and how they work.

We do know that satellites have come a long way. The very first satellite was *Sputnik*. It was sent into space in 1957 by Russian scientists. All that it had inside was a thermometer and a radio. It also had a battery for power. Today, most satellites run on the power of the sun. We can see them moving in the night sky like shooting stars. Our world would be very different without the aid of these outer-space helpers.

Name_____ Date_____

Racing through Space

Answer the questions below.

1. Which of the following statements about *Sputnik* is true?
   a. *Sputnik* was built by Americans in 1957.
   b. *Sputnik* had complicated equipment inside it.
   c. *Sputnik* was launched by Russian scientists.
   d. *Sputnik* was built in 1997.

2. Which conclusion about satellites can you draw from the article?
   a. Satellites have changed since 1957 and will keep changing.
   b. Satellites only need radios and thermometers to run.
   c. Satellites are less important than they once were.
   d. Satellites need to carry a lot of fuel on board to work.

3. Read the following sentence from the story and answer the question.

   We can see them moving in the night sky like shooting stars.

   What kind of phrase is *like shooting stars*?
   a. a metaphor
   b. a homophone
   c. alliteration
   d. a simile

4. Some satellites help find ships and

   _____ that are in trouble.

5. A _____ satellite

   watches the patterns of storms.

6. Most satellites today use _____

   _____ for power.

7. Satellites can be used to help send

   _____

   for television or radio.

8. Which of the following is a feature of a satellite?
   a. Signals can bounce off satellites.
   b. A satellite can take off and land on Earth like a plane.
   c. A jet can send a satellite into space.
   d. b. and c.

9. Which kind of satellite do you think is most important? Why do you think so? Write your answer in complete sentences.

   _____

   _____

   _____

   _____

© Carson-Dellosa

Where in the World Are You?

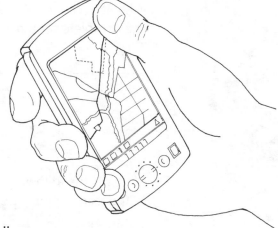

In the past, when people left home, they had to figure out where they were going on their own. They might have had a map to help them. But, the map could not tell them if they had gone off course. They might have had a compass. This showed them what direction they were going. Today, life is different. We have something called a **global positioning system**, or **GPS**. This can tell you exactly where you are in the world. How does it work?

GPS is in many new cars. There is a small *receiver*, or something that can pick up signals. It fits in your hand. The receiver doesn't do the work by itself. Global positioning satellites are in space circling the earth. There are 27 of them—24 that work together and three spares. The receiver "talks" to four satellites at a time. Each satellite sends a signal. The computer inside the receiver goes to work. It uses the placement of the satellites to pinpoint its own location. And, that is where the car is, too!

Some receivers have maps stored inside them. You can use the maps to find out where you are. Other receivers can plug into a laptop computer. The receiver keeps "talking" to the satellites. It uses their information to keep track of where the car is going.

Of course, global positioning is not just used in cars. Planes and ships use it, too. When it was first made, the system was used only by the armed forces. Today, many people and companies use the satellites.

Global positioning has changed the way people tell where they are. It has changed travel. What once was hard is now much easier, thanks to computers and satellites. Because of this amazing system, people may never get lost again!

Next Page

Where in the World Are You?

Answer the questions below.

1. What is a *receiver*? Write your answer in a complete sentence.

   _____

   _____

   _____

2. Which of the following phrases does NOT describe global positioning?

   a. uses satellites
   b. uses computers
   c. uses TVs
   d. uses signals

3.–7. Write T for true and F for false.

3. _____ The global positioning system has 29 satellites.

4. _____ The receiver talks to four satellites at a time.

5. _____ Each satellite sends a signal that tells where it is located.

6. _____ Global positioning is not used by airplanes.

7. _____ Some receivers can be plugged into a computer.

8. Which of the following phrases means the same thing as *pinpoint*?

   a. to locate precisely
   b. to handle sharply
   c. to pin to the floor
   d. petty details

9. Finish the sentences to tell three details about the GPS.

   a. It was first made for _____

      _____ .

   b. It uses satellites and

      _____ .

   c. It keeps track of where someone

      is going by sending

      _____ .

10. What is another use for global positioning that is not mentioned in the story? Write your answer in a complete sentence.

    _____

    _____

    _____

STOP

Extreme Life-Saving Machines

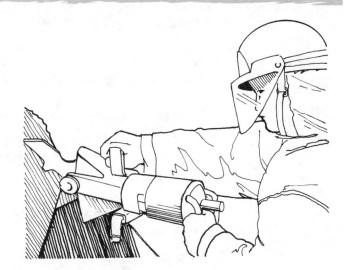

In a bad accident, a car can be crushed. A person can be trapped inside. How do workers save this person? They use a set of tools called a **cutter**, a **spreader**, and a **ram**.

All of these tools must be powerful. So, they are hooked to a type of pump that sends power through hoses to the tools. The cutter works like a giant pair of scissors. It has a huge claw on one end that closes into a point. The pump sends power to open and close the claw. The claw opens and then closes around the steel and cuts through it.

The spreader is the opposite of the cutter. It has two large arms on its end. The arms have sharp tips that touch each other. A rescue worker can push the sharp tips between two pieces of crushed metal. When the power is turned on, the two arms push apart. They pry open the metal to make an escape hole for the person inside.

The ram is the last of the three tools that are used to save lives. The ram has a different job than the other two tools. It looks like a giant *piston*, or rod, with a flat end. When the power is turned on, the ram pushes the flat end out. It can hold up something that has fallen, like the roof of a car. It can push a dashboard out of the way.

A car crash is only one time when these extreme machines are used. In earthquakes or bad storms, buildings can fall. Buildings can fall during fires, too. People might be trapped inside. A cutter, a spreader, and a ram can help get them out.

Extreme Life-Saving Machines

Answer the questions below.

1. Read the following sentences from the story and answer the question.

   When the power is turned on, the two arms push apart. They pry open the metal to make an escape hole for the person inside.

   A phrase that means the same thing as *pry open* is—
   a. push together.
   b. pull apart.
   c. push along.
   d. squeeze.

2. The tool that lets workers push something out of the way is the—
   a. spreader.
   b. cutter.
   c. ram.
   d. ladder.

3. How do these tools get their power?
   a. from a battery
   b. from a type of lever
   c. from a type of pump
   d. none of the above

4. The author writes about using the three life-saving tools in all of the following events EXCEPT—
   a. a fire.
   b. an earthquake.
   c. a skating accident.
   d. a car accident.

5. The cutter works like—
   a. a piston.
   b. a bottle opener.
   c. a hammer.
   d. a pair of scissors.

6. Which of the following sentences BEST states the main idea of the story?
   a. Three machine-powered tools help workers save lives in different kinds of accidents.
   b. The spreader pushes metal apart to make an escape hole.
   c. It is a good thing that we have tools to help save lives.
   d. The ram pushes crushed car parts, like dashboards and steering wheels, out of the way.

7. Why are the cutter, spreader, and ram important machines? Write your answer in complete sentences.

   _____

   _____

   _____

   _____

   _____

Ice Monsters

Have you ever watched an ice hockey game? How about an Olympic skating event? From time to time, you'll see big machines scoot onto the ice. They go slowly back and forth. Then, they drive off again. What are they doing? How do they work?

The machines are **ice resurfacers**. The first one was invented by a man named Frank Zamboni. Frank owned a big *ice rink*, a place where people could go to skate. After many people skate on ice, it gets cut and chipped. Skaters can trip over cuts in the ice. They can fall. So, the ice needs to be *groomed*, or smoothed. In the past, a driver would pull a tractor over the ice to smooth it. Workers would walk over the ice, sweeping away the shavings. Then, they would spread water over the ice and let it freeze. It took a long time. Frank Zamboni was sure he could think of a better way to do this.

He did! His ice resurfacer is like a big truck. It pushes a sharp blade over the ice. This removes the damaged top layer of the ice. A huge screw inside the truck comes down and gathers the ice shavings. At the same time, a water tank spreads water over the ice. The ice is washed. Extra water is sucked back into the tank. In the last step, a giant towel spreads hot water over the ice. This makes the top of the ice very smooth. One machine does all of this work.

You can see Frank Zamboni's amazing machines at many ice rinks. They are used during ice hockey games. At the Olympics, the machines zip onto the ice between skating events. What once took hours now takes minutes, thanks to this fascinating ice machine.

Next Page

Ice Monsters

Answer the questions below.

1. Look at the chain of events that describes how an ice resurfacer works and answer the question.

> The ice resurfacer cuts the top of the ice with a blade.

↓

> A screw inside the truck gathers the ice shavings.

↓

> Extra water is sucked into the truck.

↓

> Hot water is spread over the top of the ice.

Which step is missing?

a. Ice is chopped up and hauled away in another truck.
b. The ice is cut into squares.
c. The ice is washed.
d. The ice is melted.

2. Read the following sentence from the story and answer the question.

At the Olympics, the machines zip onto the ice between the skating events.

Which of the following words could replace *zip* in the sentence?

a. lumber
b. speed
c. trot
d. wander

3. Which of the following sentences about the ice resurfacer is a fact and NOT an opinion?

a. The ice resurfacer is the greatest invention for sports in the last 100 years.
b. The ice resurfacer does work that several workers used to take hours to do.
c. The ice resurfacer is fun to watch.
d. The ice resurfacer is the best thing about ice hockey games.

4. Why is the ice resurfacer necessary?

a. When people skate on ice, ice skates chop and cut it.
b. In ice sports, ice needs to have a smooth top.
c. Cuts in the ice can make skaters trip and fall.
d. all of the above

5. Describe one feature of the ice resurfacer. Write your answer in a complete sentence.

_____

_____

_____

_____

STOP

Quack, Quack!

Ducks can go from land to water. That is true of the bird. It is also true of the trucks and cars called **ducks**. You may have seen a duck in a spy movie. But, this water-to-land transportation is real.

Ducks were used during World War II. The first ducks were big, heavy trucks shaped like tanks. The huge trucks could take troops and supplies from a ship to the land. The trucks could drive onto land from the water. They were big and slow, but they helped keep soldiers safe.

After the war, some people in the United States bought ducks. They were used for tourist rides. In cities like Philadelphia, Pennsylvania, you can ride in a duck. The duck takes you to sights on land. Then, it drives into the water!

These old army trucks are not the only ducks out there. People have invented new ducks—fast sports-car ducks that are more like spy-movie cars. These ducks are small and sleek. They can move very fast on land—up to 100 miles per hour. In order to go in the water, the cars must go down a slope or a beach. Once a duck is in the water, the wheels flip under the car. It becomes a boat! In the water, these cool cars can go between 30 and 40 miles per hour. That is a lot faster than the old World War II ducks, which can only travel about 6 miles per hour in the water.

It would be exciting to own a sports-car duck. Just having it for fun is not its only possible use. Some people are working to make the new ducks into ambulances. In cities like Seattle, Washington, where there is a lot of water and many islands, an ambulance that could speed from land to water could save lives.

Conversions

100 miles per hour = 160.93 kilometers per hour
30 miles per hour = 48.28 kilometers per hour
40 miles per hour = 64.37 kilometers per hour
6 miles per hour = 9.66 kilometers per hour

Next Page

Name _____ Date _____

Quack, Quack!

Answer the questions below.

1.–5. Match each word to its antonym.

1. _____ fast   a. crawl

2. _____ huge   b. boring

3. _____ exciting   c. light

4. _____ heavy   d. tiny

5. _____ speed   e. slow

6. Read the following sentence from the story and answer the question.

   These ducks are small and sleek.

   What is a synonym for *sleek*?
   a. clunky
   b. dull
   c. streamlined
   d. silly

7. Which of the following sentences from the story is an opinion?
   a. After the war, some people in the United States bought ducks.
   b. Ducks were used during World War II.
   c. It would be exciting to own a sports-car duck.
   d. The trucks could drive onto land from the water.

8. Fill in the blanks to finish the following sentences.

   a. Some ducks are used as rides for

      _____.

   b. To get into the water, sports-car

      ducks must go down a

      _____.

   c. One life-saving use of a duck

      might be as an _____.

9. Circle the correct word or phrase in parentheses to complete each sentence.

   a. A duck (**is** , **is not**) a submarine that can go on land.

   b. Sports-car ducks can go up to (**10** , **25** , **40**) miles per hour in the water.

   c. Ducks were used during (**World War I** , **World War II**).

   d. The sports-car duck's (**brakes** , **wheels** , **windows**) flip under the car in the water.

Faster Than a Speeding Bullet

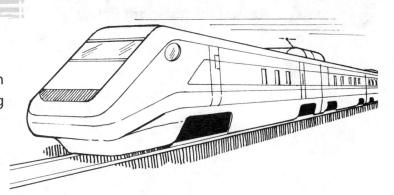

Can a train ride be as fast as a plane ride? It can if you are rocketing along in a **bullet train**. This is an extreme form of train travel. It is getting more popular every day.

Bullet trains were first used in Japan. The trains were planned in 1957. They started running in 1959. Before the bullet train, it took seven hours to go from one end of Japan to the other. The same ride on the bullet train took about 3.5 hours. When the first bullet train started to run, it was the fastest train in the world.

But, even that first bullet train would look slow today! Today, most bullet trains can run between 200 and 300 miles per hour. Newer models can be even faster. Japan is not the only country with these super trains. Many countries in Europe now have them, too. In many of these countries, it is now faster to take the train than it is to fly in a plane.

How do bullet trains go so fast? There are three things that help these trains speed along. One is the shape of the train. It is shaped with a long, flat nose in front and has low cars. This helps the wind flow over the train. The wind does not slow the train down. Another thing that helps are tracks with no sharp curves. All of the curves are long and smooth, so that the train does not have to slow down as it travels. Finally, the special bullet-train tracks never cross roads or other train tracks. The train never has to stop for other traffic.

What does it feel like to be on a bullet train? The speed is so fast that you cannot see anything outside the windows. The land is a blur. Most people say it feels more like flying in a plane than being on the ground.

Conversions
200 miles per hour = 321.87 kilometers per hour
300 miles per hour = 482.8 kilometers per hour

Name _____ Date _____

Faster Than a Speeding Bullet

Answer the questions below.

1. The first bullet train was in the

   country of _____ .

2. Bullet trains can now travel between

   _____ miles per hour and

   _____ miles per hour.

3. Today, there are many bullet trains

   in _____ ,

   as well as Asia.

4. Traveling in a bullet train feels more

   like being in a _____

   than a train.

5. The first bullet train started running

   in the year _____ .

6.–9. Write T for true and F for false.

6. _____ One reason the bullet train
   can go so fast is that it has
   low cars.

7. _____ The nose of a bullet train is
   high and peaked.

8. _____ When you ride in a bullet
   train, the land outside is just
   a blur.

9. _____ The first bullet train was
   twice as fast as an
   old-fashioned train.

10. Read the following sentences from
    the story and answer the question.

    Can a train ride be as fast as a plane
    ride? It can if you are rocketing
    along in a bullet train.

    Which of the following words is a
    synonym for *rocketing*?
    a. speeding
    b. racing
    c. wandering
    d. a. and b.

11. Would you like to ride on a bullet
    train? Why or why not? Write your
    answer in complete sentences.

    _____

    _____

    _____

    _____

Sweet Machines

Doughnuts have been a favorite treat for hundreds of years. It was the Dutch who first made "oily cakes." Little balls of dough were rolled by hand. They were dropped one by one into a kettle of oil, but they didn't cook all of the way through. So, Dutch cooks filled the little cakes with raisins or jam. Each doughnut was made by hand.

As time passed, people grew to love doughnuts more and more. Today, **doughnut machines** make thousands of the treats at a time. How do machines make so many of these sweet treats?

One machine *stamps out*, or shapes, doughnuts into their round shape. After that, the doughnuts go for a long ride on a moving belt. First, the belt carries the doughnuts into a warming oven. This oven makes the yeast in the dough puff up, or *rise*. Doughnuts are not baked in the oven, though. Doughnuts are fried, not baked. The days of the big kettle are over. Instead, doughnuts ride into an oil bath. They float in the hot oil and then land on the belt again once they are cooked. On some machines, the belt flips the doughnuts over so that they will cook on both sides. Other machines spray hot oil over the doughnuts to cook the tops.

The ride is not over yet. Doughnuts are sweet treats because they usually have some kind of sugar on them. Some doughnuts are *glazed*, or covered, with a clear sheet of sugar and milk. These doughnuts go for a ride through a waterfall of glaze! The sheet of glaze coats the doughnuts. Then, the doughnuts have to cool before they are sold.

Other doughnuts are filled with cream or jam, just like they were hundreds of years ago. These doughnuts ride to another machine. Someone pushes each doughnut against a pipe that pumps filling into it. Frosted doughnuts are dipped in vanilla or chocolate frosting before they ride out on the belt to be packed in boxes.

Next Page

Name_____ Date_____

Sweet Machines

Answer the questions below.

1. Which of the following sentences is an opinion?

   a. The Dutch invented doughnuts.
   b. Doughnuts are the best breakfast treat of all time.
   c. Today, most doughnuts are made by machines.
   d. Doughnuts ride on belts as they are cooked and frosted.

2. Which of the following sentences is NOT true?

   a. Machines today make one doughnut at a time.
   b. Doughnuts used to be made in kettles.
   c. Many people love doughnuts.
   d. Doughnuts used to be called "oily cakes."

3. Read the following sentences from the story and answer the question.

   First, the belt carries the doughnuts into a warming oven. This oven makes the yeast in the dough puff up, or *rise*.

   What is another food that has to *rise* before it is cooked?

   a. steak
   b. butter
   c. salad
   d. bread

4. What is *glaze*?

   a. a mixture of sugar and candy
   b. a mixture of yeast and milk
   c. a mixture of frosting and jam
   d. a mixture of sugar and milk

5. Which of the following is NOT a step in doughnut making?

   a. rising in a warming oven
   b. floating in an oil bath
   c. hanging on lines to dry
   d. being packed into boxes

6. Do you like doughnuts? Why or why not? Write your answer in complete sentences.

   _____

   _____

   _____

   _____

   _____

   _____

Touch the Vote

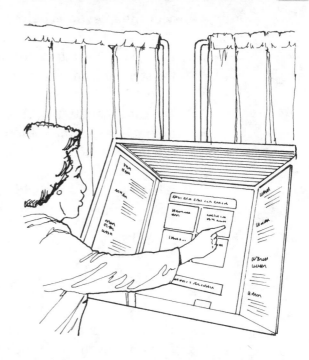

Long ago, Americans voted by drawing an X on a piece of paper next to a name. Then, the pieces of paper were counted by hand. As the country grew, workers had to find new ways to count every person's vote. Today, there are many different voting systems in the United States. Some people still use paper ballots. Most of these are punched with a sharp piece of metal to show the vote. In other places, people vote with a touch-screen machine.

The **touch-screen voting machine** is a type of computer. It has a special screen. In most of the voting machines, there are two pieces of glass. Between the pieces of glass is a *sensor*, a tiny piece that "feels" the touch of a finger. It is like the sensor inside a computer mouse. The sensor sends a message to a computer card. When someone touches the screen to vote, the sensor tells the computer card the name that the voter picked. The card changes that choice into a language that the computer can understand.

Inside the voting machine, special software keeps track of the votes. Each machine counts its votes. In some places, the information from all of the machines is sent to one place to be added again.

New kinds of voting machines will make it faster to total the votes. But, could there still be problems? Some people worry that the newest machines do not have a *paper trail*. This is a report, printed on paper, that shows the votes that the computer tracked. It is used to check votes. Other people worry that the sensors under the glass might stop working. Or, maybe the computer could *crash*, or quit working, during voting. All of these problems are things that people in the United States will need to fix to make sure that every vote gets counted.

Next Page

Touch the Vote

Answer the questions below.

1. Read the following sentence from the story and answer the question.

   The card changes that choice into a language that the computer can understand.

   What is a word that could be used in place of *changes* in the sentence?
   a. translates
   b. transports
   c. trades
   d. traps

2. The story mentions all of the following features of touch-screen voting EXCEPT—
   a. the sensor inside the glass screen.
   b. the computer card.
   c. the computer software.
   d. the voting booth.

3. What is a *paper trail*?
   a. litter in a voting place
   b. a paper report that is used to check the votes
   c. papers handed out to tell about the voting choices
   d. none of the above

4.–6. Write T for true and F for false.

4. _____ During touch-screen voting, someone writes each vote on paper to check the computer.

5. _____ Ballots were once marked with an X next to the voter's choice.

6. _____ Sensors are used in touch-screen voting and in a computer mouse.

7. Based on the story, what can you infer about the difference between paper ballots and touch-screen voting?
   a. Touch-screen voting is faster but may cause other kinds of problems.
   b. Paper ballots are the best way to vote.
   c. Voting is not important in the United States.
   d. Touch-screen voting is based on punch cards.

8. Describe one possible problem with touch-screen voting. Write your answer in complete sentences.

   _____

   _____

   _____

   _____

Fly Me to the Moon

Would you like to fly into space? In the past, only astronauts could do that. Governments chose the people who went into space. Someday soon, people may be able to take vacations in space! That's the hope of the crew working on **SpaceShipOne**.

SpaceShipOne is like an airplane with a rocket engine. The special engine gives the spacecraft *thrust*, which is a big boost upward. A big airplane, called the *White Knight*, carries *SpaceShipOne* into the air. When the *White Knight* releases *SpaceShipOne*, the spacecraft's engine mixes a special type of gas with rubber. This mixture causes a reaction that sends the spaceship high enough to go into orbit.

People working on *SpaceShipOne* have to fix some problems. When it first takes off, the thrust can make it roll in the air. Keeping the spacecraft on course is also hard. The higher it goes, the stronger the wind. The wind blows the spaceship off course. But, workers feel that soon these problems will be fixed.

What will spacecrafts like *SpaceShipOne* be used for? For now, they will just make trips into space. People will pay thousands of dollars to fly high enough to see the stars. One day, there may even be hotels that orbit the earth. Space stations could have rooms where tourists can stay. Imagine spending a vacation in a room in space!

Maybe spacecrafts like these will someday travel to other planets. People may make colonies there. They will need to go back and forth to visit Earth. Spacecrafts like *SpaceShipOne* could play a part in those plans.

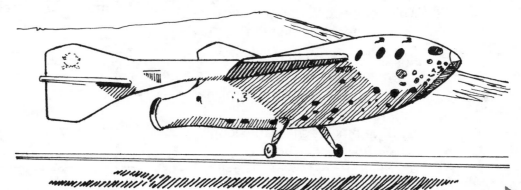

Next Page ▶

Fly Me to the Moon

Answer the questions below.

1. Read the following sentence from the story and answer the question.

   The wind blows the spaceship off course.

   What does *off course* mean?

   a. away from Earth
   b. off the path it is supposed to travel
   c. off the map so that it cannot be charted
   d. away from space

2. Which sentence BEST summarizes the main idea of the story?

   a. Private spacecrafts with rocket engines are not perfect yet.
   b. Private spacecrafts are better than rockets for travel.
   c. Space stations may someday be used as hotels.
   d. Space travel may soon be possible for many people, not just astronauts.

3. Which of the following sentences from the story is an opinion?

   a. Maybe spacecrafts like these will someday travel to other planets.
   b. *SpaceShipOne* is like an airplane with a rocket engine.
   c. Governments chose the people who went into space.
   d. When *SpaceShipOne* first takes off, the thrust can make it roll in the air.

4. What is the meaning of *thrust* as it is used in this story?

   a. a big boost upward
   b. to push into someone's hands
   c. the main point of something
   d. none of the above

5. *SpaceShipOne* is flown into the air by a big airplane called _____

   _____ .

6. Tourists may someday have rooms in a _____ .

7. *SpaceShipOne's* thrust is created by mixing _____

   _____ with rubber.

8. Do you think that people will live in colonies on other planets someday? Why or why not? Write your answer in complete sentences.

   _____

   _____

   _____

   _____

STOP

Flying and Spying

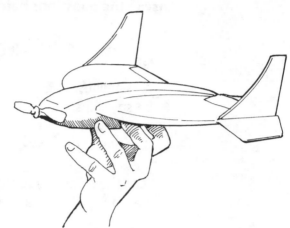

In movies, spying looks like fun. But, in real life, keeping track of danger is serious business. There are machines that help with that work. A **spy plane** is one of these machines.

There are many types of spy planes. Each kind does a different type of work. One of the most common spy planes is used as a listening machine. These planes fly over or near countries that people want to watch. The plane has radar. The plane also has sensors and *dish antennas*, like those used for TV. Both the top and the bottom of the plane have these dishes. With these "ears," the plane picks up several kinds of information. It can "hear" satellite messages. It can "listen" to radio messages from ships. It can listen to telephone calls and even pick up faxes. People look at this information to see if it contains anything important.

Other planes take pictures, just like satellites do. But, airplanes can fly closer to the ground than satellites can. Pilots must be careful, though. It is against the law to fly over some countries. If the country is unfriendly, the plane might be forced to land.

Spy planes come in many sizes. The government of Israel invented tiny spy planes that fly without pilots onboard. The smallest one is called *Birdy*. It only weighs three pounds. It can even be carried in a backpack! A soldier can launch the tiny plane. The soldier uses a laptop computer to show the plane where to fly. *Birdy* can even fly through a window and take pictures inside a building! The tiny plane takes pictures that are instantly sent to the computer. Planes like these can be used to spy during battles, as well as in peacetime.

Conversion

3 pounds = 1.36 kilograms

Next Page

Flying and Spying

Answer the questions below.

1. The title, "Flying and Spying," refers to—

   a. satellites.
   b. spy ships.
   c. spy planes.
   d. none of the above

2. Read the following sentence from the story and answer the question.

   People look at this information to see if it contains anything important.

   Which of the following is a synonym for *information*?

   a. data
   b. fiction
   c. advice
   d. stories

3. Which of the following is the BEST description of the most common kind of spy plane?

   a. an airplane that gathers messages and carries them home again
   b. an airplane that listens to and collects radio messages, telephone calls, and other information
   c. an airplane that flies very fast over other countries
   d. an airplane that can be sent to pick up information from other countries

4. Why would spy planes take pictures if satellites can do it?

   _____

   _____

5. Write three words or phrases from the story that describe the spy plane from Israel.

   a. _____

   b. _____

   c. _____

6. Which of the following features might a spy plane have?

   a. sensors to pick up messages
   b. dish antennas
   c. cameras
   d. all of the above

7. Do you think it is important to have spy planes? Why or why not? Write your answer in complete sentences.

   _____

   _____

   _____

The Machines That Found *Titanic*

The great ship *Titanic* sank in 1912. For over 70 years, no one could find the wreck on the ocean floor. Then, an explorer named Dr. Robert Ballard decided to look for *Titanic*. He had three special machines that helped him make history.

The first machine was one that Dr. Ballard invented. It is called **Argo**. Argo is like a big sled. It was towed underwater below Dr. Ballard's ship. It uses sonar to look at the ocean floor. Sonar scans the sea floor. It bounces sound off the floor. If the sound waves bounce off a shape, that shape shows on a screen. Other explorers had used sonar to help them look for *Titanic* in the past. Dr. Ballard thought that he needed a closer look. Argo gave him that look because it also has cameras. It sent pictures to the ship where Dr. Ballard and his team were waiting. On September 1, 1985, Argo found something big. It was not a rock or a part of the sea floor. It was a boiler from the engine of *Titanic*. The great ship was found!

Dr. Ballard was ready to go down to look at *Titanic*. To do that, he used another special machine. This one was called **Alvin**. *Alvin* is a small, round submarine that holds three people. It was built to work in very deep water. *Titanic* was 12,000 feet under the water. It took Dr. Ballard and two other crew members 2.5 hours just to go that deep into the sea! Because they had *Alvin*, they knew they could go that deep. Unlike other submarines, *Alvin* can land on the sea floor. It has special lights to help the explorers see. And, it holds another machine for more help.

Make a prediction.

What do you think the author will write about next? Circle your answer.

how *Titanic* sank   the third machine   *Alvin's* other features

Conversion

12,000 feet = 3,657.6 meters

Name_____ Date_____

Answer the following questions based on what you read on page 31. Then, finish reading the story at the bottom of the page.

1. What is an antonym for *special*?
   a. interesting
   b. unusual
   c. ordinary
   d. different

2. How did the explorers first know they had found *Titanic*?
   a. *Alvin* sent them pictures of the ship.
   b. They went to the floor of the sea and saw the wreck.
   c. They had a map that showed them where the ship was.
   d. *Argo* sent them pictures of part of *Titanic's* engine.

3. Describe Argo. Write your answer in complete sentences.

   _____

   _____

   _____

4. What was the name of the submarine that the explorers used?
   a. Argo
   b. *Titanic*
   c. *Alvin*
   d. Alice

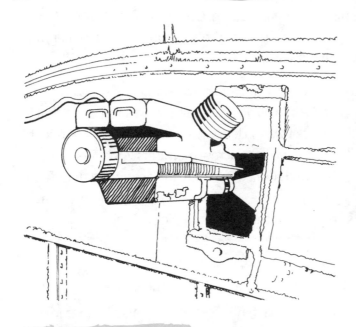

Conversion

300 feet = 91.44 meters

The third machine used to help explore the *Titanic* was called **Jason, Junior**. The crew called it **JJ** for short. JJ is a little, floating robot. JJ rides inside *Alvin* in a space called "the garage." When Dr. Ballard opened the garage doors, JJ floated out in front of *Alvin*. The robot is linked to *Alvin* by a 300-foot cable. Dr. Ballard and other crew members could make JJ move any way that they wanted. The *Titanic* wreck is too deep for divers to explore. The deep sea is not safe for humans. JJ was small enough to go through windows and doors on the ship. Dr. Ballard sent JJ into cabins. He sent the little robot down *Titanic's* Grand Staircase. It sent back pictures that the explorers were able to study.

Next Page ➡

The Machines That Found *Titanic*

Answer the questions below.

5. Why did the explorers need JJ?

   a. It was not safe for them to dive and go into *Titanic* themselves.
   b. They could not get out of the submarine to explore.
   c. They needed to see inside the ship, and JJ has cameras to take pictures.
   d. all of the above

6. Read the following sentence from the story and answer the question.

   JJ rides inside *Alvin* in a space called "the garage."

   What happened when the garage doors were opened?

   a. JJ drifted away.
   b. JJ floated ahead of *Alvin*, linked by a cable.
   c. *Alvin* used the garage space for another machine.
   d. The crew used JJ to pull themselves back to the top of the sea.

7. Why do you think *Alvin* could not go inside *Titanic*?

   a. *Alvin* was too big.
   b. *Alvin* could not be controlled.
   c. *Alvin* could not go up and down.
   d. *Alvin* would not be able to get out.

8. Which of the following is an opinion?

   a. Argo uses both sonar and cameras.
   b. *Alvin* was built to work in the deep sea.
   c. Finding *Titanic* was the most important discovery ever.
   d. Dr. Ballard invented Argo.

9. Which of the following is NOT true?

   a. *Titanic* was found at a depth of 12,000 feet.
   b. Other ships used sonar to look for *Titanic* in the past.
   c. JJ took pictures inside cabins on the ship.
   d. Dr. Ballard was the first person to look for the wreck of *Titanic*.

10. List three details that describe *Alvin's* features.

   a. _____

   _____

   b. _____

   _____

   c. _____

   _____

A World of Robots

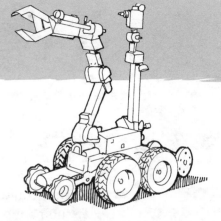

For many years, people have told stories about **robots**. These machines can help us live better lives. You can see robots in movies. Sometimes, they act like friends. They can do many different things. The first movie robot was shown in a film made in 1924. In the movie, robots were made to free humans from boring tasks. Is a world of robots just a dream?

Robots are now a part of real life. But, robots have only been around for about 50 years. Before robots could be made, scientists had to invent a type of "brain" for them. That happened when people created computer chips. Many robots also have sensors inside them. These help robots "see" light and "feel" walls or things in their paths. Sensors also help people give commands to robots. A robot can be told to move in one way or another. By moving in these ways, a robot can do a job. What kinds of jobs do people give to robots?

Just like the robots in the 1924 movie, robots today can do things over and over again without getting tired. They paint things. They make car parts. They put food in boxes. They build computer chips, too!

Robots also have jobs that are filled with danger. People use robots to take apart bombs. Robots can crawl into pipes to see if something is blocking the flow of water. Scientists have even built a robot that can walk into a volcano to get rock samples. And, robots have helped explore deep, underwater places and very cold places where humans cannot go. The Mars rover is a robot that works on the planet Mars. What other jobs could people give to robots in the future?

? Make a prediction.

What do you think the author will write about next?

Next Page

Answer the following questions based on what you read on page 34. Then, finish reading the story at the bottom of the page.

1. Read the following sentence from the story and answer the question.

   Sensors also help people give commands to robots.

   Which of the following is a synonym for *commands*?

   a. help
   b. orders
   c. beginnings
   d. approvals

2. What helps a robot "see" or "feel" things?

   a. samples
   b. dreams
   c. sensors
   d. fingers

3. When was the movie made that first featured a robot on the screen?

   a. 1942
   b. 1920
   c. 1926
   d. 1924

Scientists think that they will keep building smarter robots so that we will have more of them working for us. Scientists are already working on robots that can mow lawns or vacuum floors. Maybe someday soon, we will have robots that do all of our chores for us!

Even further in the future, we will have robots that know how to handle different objects around them. These robots will know that a book cannot break easily, but an egg can. They will be able to learn new things. They will be able to talk and listen to people. They will know when people are happy or sad. They will be able to cook, talk on the phone, and write. With robots like these, our lives may become more and more like the science fiction movies of the past.

Next Page

Name _____   Date _____

A World of Robots

Answer the questions below.

4.–7. Write T for true and F for false.

4. _____ Robots can get tired
doing their jobs.

5. _____ Scientists made a robot
that walks into volcanoes.

6. _____ Robots can paint cars
in factories.

7. _____ Robots have computer
chips that work like brains.

8. Read the following sentence from
the story and answer the question.

Robots also have jobs that are filled
with danger.

What word could be used in place of
filled with danger?

a. secure
b. daring
c. distant
d. dangerous

9. According to the story, which of the
following things can robots do?

a. go to very cold places
b. travel to Mars
c. pack boxes
d. all of the above

10. List three things that robots may be
able to do in the future.

a. _____

b. _____

c. _____

11. Explain how your life might change
if you had a robot. Write your
answer in complete sentences.

_____

_____

_____

_____

_____

_____

_____

STOP

A New Vision

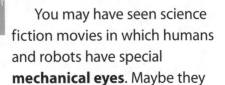

You may have seen science fiction movies in which humans and robots have special **mechanical eyes**. Maybe they help the hero see farther or better. Could these amazing eyes someday be available in real life? Could a type of camera or telescope help people see? Yes, because cameras and telescopes have lenses just like eyes do.

How does the lens in an eye work? The lens helps to focus light. When an eye looks at things that are far away or close up, the eye lens changes shape. The lens curves as it looks at things that are nearby. It flattens as it looks at things that are far away. A camera lens changes, too. In both cases, this change helps keep pictures from being blurry. The lens can stop working in a human eye. As people get older, it is harder for their eye lenses to change shape. This makes it harder to see.

Doctors in the Netherlands worked to make new lenses for eyes. The lenses were like the lenses in a camera. The doctors invented a lens that can be put over the *pupil*, or black center, of an eye. It is held down on each side with hinges. This lens helps people who can only see things that are nearby, not far away. After the new lenses are added to their eyes, they can see things far away, too. That's because the lens zooms in and out, just like the lens on a camera.

Another idea to help eyes came from the telescope. Today, doctors can put a tiny telescope inside a human eye. It makes things look bigger. The telescope is put into one eye for seeing close up. The other eye is left without a telescope so that it can see far away. This is used to help people who are losing their sight. With ideas like these, what changes do you think might be in the future for the human eye?

Make a prediction.

What do you think the author will write about next? Circle your answer.

the history of medicine   how the eye works   future help for eyes

Next Page →

Answer the following questions based on what you read on page 37. Then, finish reading the story at the bottom of the page.

1. An eye lens helps to focus _____ .

2. Doctors in the _____ worked to make new lenses for the human eye.

3. The black center of an eye is called the _____ .

4. When an eye looks at something that is nearby, it _____ .

5. Some doctors invented a new eye lens that is held in place with—

   a. clamps.
   b. ropes.
   c. hinges.
   d. gears.

6. Read the following sentence from the story and answer the question.

   You may have seen science fiction movies where humans and robots have special mechanical eyes.

   What is the meaning of the word *mechanical* as it is used in this sentence?

   a. works like a mechanic
   b. works with levers or pulleys
   c. works like a machine
   d. not working well

Scientists are now working to use a type of camera to help people who have become blind. They are testing a tiny computer chip. This chip would be planted into the lens of a blind eye. After that, the person would wear special glasses. The glasses would have a tiny video camera inside. The camera would take in light and "see" something. It would send that picture to a screen inside the glasses. The chip would read it. Then, it would tell the person's brain how to "see" the picture. This system could help blind people see large shapes and light. This would be an exciting step in helping people who have lost their sight to see again. Someday, we may be able to correct many human eyes with ideas like these.

A New Vision

Answer the questions below.

7. Read the following sentence from the story and answer the question.

   This would be an exciting step in helping people who have lost their sight to see again.

   Is this a fact or an opinion?

   _____

8. Which of the following sentences BEST summarizes the story?

   a. Scientists are using special cameras and telescopes to help people.
   b. Scientists are using special cameras and telescopes to help people see better.
   c. Someday, scientists will be able to help blind people see.
   d. Eyes and cameras both have lenses.

9. How does the camera lens with hinges help people to see better?

   a. It zooms in and out like a camera lens.
   b. It sends a message to a computer chip in the brain.
   c. It makes the eye clear again.
   d. none of the above

10. What can be put into the eye of a person who is losing his sight?

    a. a new camera held in place with hinges
    b. a tiny telescope
    c. a microchip
    d. a colored lens

11. Look at the chain of events below and answer the question.

A tiny computer chip is planted into the lens of a blind eye.

    ↓

A little video camera sends a picture to the screen.

    ↓

The chip sees the picture.

    ↓

The chip tells the person's brain how to read the picture.

    Which step is missing?

    a. The person must wear bright colors.
    b. The video camera has to be turned on.
    c. The person has to wear special glasses.
    d. The person's brain sends a message back to the chip.

Inside a Computer

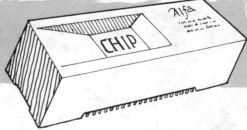

Computers have many jobs to do! There are computers that do simple things, as well as computers that do hard jobs. Computers come in all shapes and sizes. But, the most interesting part of a computer is the inside.

A computer is run by a *CPU*, or *central processing unit*. It is like the computer's brain. The CPU stores a computer's memory. All of the programs on a computer "talk" to the CPU to get it to help them. The computer's *operating system* works to sort all of the different requests.

An operating system is like a traffic officer for a computer. It sorts the jobs that the computer has to do. It gives memory to each program and tells the different programs how to work with each other. A computer cannot run without its operating system. It keeps the computer from getting *overloaded*, or too busy.

Many things have computers in them. But, not all things that have a computer need an operating system. A coffee maker is a good example. It has a computer inside it but no operating system because it only does one thing. It has a timer that tells it when to turn on and off. Because it only has one job, it does not need an operating system. Operating systems are for things that have more than one job.

When you want to run a program, the operating system sends a signal to the CPU. It sets a time to *launch*, or start, the program. Then, it remembers all of the things about the file that you make. It keeps track of what time you started the file, how the file is linked to the program, and what time you finished.

All of these complicated things work when your computer is running well. Sometimes though, computers get "sick."

Make a prediction.

What do you think the story will describe next?

_____

Name _____ Date _____

Answer the following questions based on what you read on page 40. Then, finish reading the story at the bottom of the page.

1. Write three phrases that describe the operating system's job.

   a. _____

   b. _____

   c. _____

2. Which of the following probably does NOT have an operating system?

   a. an alarm clock
   b. a blender
   c. a microwave
   d. all of the above

3. Read the following sentence from the story and answer the question.

   An operating system is like a traffic officer for a computer.

   What kind of phrase is *like a traffic officer for a computer*?

   a. a metaphor
   b. hyperbole
   c. alliteration
   d. a simile

Computer programs do not run all of the time. As soon as someone touches the keyboard, the operating system finds a place to store the work. The operating system talks to the program the whole time someone is using it. But, when a computer has a *virus*, or bad program, something else happens. A virus is a piece of software. It hurts the computer by attaching itself to a program. Every time someone runs that program, the virus runs, too. It makes copies of itself and attaches the copies to other programs. This confuses the operating system. It cannot talk to the programs anymore. The virus takes over. It does not listen to the operating system. Soon, the whole computer can shut down.

There are ways to get rid of viruses, but it can be tricky. When someone is able to get rid of a virus, the operating system can go back to work. It goes back to handling the traffic of the busy computer!

Next Page ➤

Inside a Computer

Answer the questions below.

4. A virus is a piece of _____

   that sticks to a _____ .

   It does not listen to the

   _____ .

5. What is kept in a CPU?

   a. computer memory
   b. cures for viruses
   c. a keyboard
   d. a mouse

6. Read the following sentence from the story and answer the question.

   It keeps the computer from getting *overloaded*, or too busy.

   Which of the following is a synonym for *overloaded*?

   a. overheard
   b. overhauled
   c. overworked
   d. overhanded

7. What does it mean to *launch* software?

   a. shut down
   b. correct
   c. fix
   d. none of the above

8. Read the following sentences from the story and answer the question.

   This confuses the operating system. It cannot talk to the programs anymore. The virus takes over. It does not listen to the operating system. Soon, the whole computer can shut down.

   What can you infer from this description?

   a. The virus stops the talk between the operating system and the programs.
   b. The virus does not hurt the CPU.
   c. When the operating system cannot do its job, the computer stops working.
   d. a. and c.

9. Would a TV need an operating system? Why or why not? Write your answer in complete sentences.

   _____

   _____

   _____

   _____

   _____

Mars or Bust

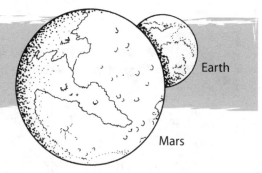

Earth

Mars

Mars is an extreme planet. It is dry, rocky, and cold. It has deep canyons and lots of dust. It has strange weather patterns that include big dust storms. So, robots made to explore Mars have to be tough. They must be able to keep working in strange weather. They have to move on rocky ground. That's what **Mars rovers** do.

Mars rovers look like toy trucks on roller skates. But, they are much more than that. The flat body of a rover keeps the computer inside it safe. The flat deck of the body lets cameras sit on the top. A rover has a heating system inside its body, too. That is because it gets very cold at night on Mars. The temperature can be -140°F! The entire rover body would freeze if it did not have its own onboard heating system.

Like other robots, a rover has sensors. They let it know where it is going on Mars. It sends information to Earth about the ground it is traveling over. It "talks" to a computer that is run by the flight team. The team tells the rover where to go and how fast to travel.

A rover's "head" is a set of cameras. It sits on a *mast*, or pole. The mast lets the cameras take pictures from higher off the ground. The cameras also move in a circle so that they can take pictures from every angle. They send both black-and-white and color pictures to the computer. They are not the only cameras on the rover. A rover also has four cameras close to the ground so that it can "see" if it will fall over or get stuck. Another camera is on the rover's arm. The arm can swing down to take close-up shots of the dirt and rocks on Mars. All of these pictures help scientists learn more about the planet. Rovers have other jobs, too.

Make a prediction.

What do you think the story will describe next?

_____

Conversion

-140˚F = -95.56˚C

Name_____ Date_____

Answer the following questions based on what you read on page 43. Then, finish reading the story at the bottom of the page.

1. The first part of the story describes all of the following EXCEPT—
   a. how the Mars rovers stay warm.
   b. how the Mars rovers will return to Earth.
   c. what it is like on Mars.
   d. how the Mars rovers take pictures.

2. Why does the author start the story by telling what it is like on Mars?
   a. so that the reader will understand how hard it is for the rovers to travel on Mars
   b. so that the reader will know more about our solar system
   c. so that the reader will compare life on Mars to life on Earth
   d. so that the reader will understand how easy it is for the rovers to move around

3. Why do rovers have cameras on their arms?
   a. They have cameras on their arms so that they can see where they are going.
   b. They have cameras on their arms so that they can take close-up pictures of dirt and rocks.
   c. They have cameras on their arms so that they can take pictures from high above the ground.
   d. none of the above.

4. Write one sentence that describes a Mars rover.

   _____

   _____

What other jobs are rovers doing on Mars? They have testing instruments inside their bodies. When a rover picks up a rock or takes pictures of the ground, measurements are taken. There are magnets in rovers. These help them pick up certain kinds of dust. Rovers also take temperature readings.

Rovers stay on Mars forever. As the planet turns away from Earth and the sun, more dust falls over the rovers. This makes it harder for them to move. The robots' batteries start to get weak. As the cold planet takes over, Rovers just stop working. By the time that happens, scientists will have already collected years of data from the little robots. Rovers teach us many details that we never knew about our neighboring planet.

Next Page

Mars or Bust

Answer the questions below.

5. Which of the following sentences BEST summarizes the story?
    a. The Mars rovers are on Mars to take photographs.
    b. The Mars rovers are robots that are gathering information about the planet Mars.
    c. The Mars rovers have to move carefully because of the rocky ground and dust storms.
    d. The Mars rovers are robots.

6. Read the following sentence from the story and answer the question.

    So, robots made to explore Mars have to be tough.

    What is an antonym for *tough* as it is used in this sentence?

    a. strong
    b. calm
    c. rough
    d. weak

7. According to the story, which of the following things is something that a Mars rover CAN do?

    a. take measurements
    b. jump across canyons
    c. fly
    d. float in water

8. According to the story, which of the following is NOT a feature of a Mars rover?

    a. a mast that holds cameras
    b. a flat body
    c. a peaked roof
    d. an arm that moves

9. Mars rovers stop working when—

    a. more dust falls on their bodies.
    b. their batteries get weak.
    c. they can't stay warm enough to keep working.
    d. all of the above

10. Why do you think scientists leave the rovers on Mars and do not bring them back to Earth? Write your answer in complete sentences.

     _____

     _____

     _____

     _____

     _____

     _____

     _____

What Is a Hybrid?

A *hybrid* is made by putting two things together. A **hybrid car** takes the gas engine of a regular car and combines it with an electric motor that runs on a battery. That way, it can get its power from more than one place.

There are different ways of making hybrid cars. In one kind of hybrid, the gas engine does not drive the car at all. Sometimes, it makes the spark that starts the electric motor. In other cases, it charges the battery. Then, the battery runs the car.

There is another way to make a hybrid. In this car, the gas engine and the electric motor switch back and forth. Sometimes, the gas engine is running the car; sometimes, the electric motor is. In other hybrid cars, the two power sources have different jobs. For example, the electric motor might start the car but not run it.

There are many different designs. But, all hybrid cars are complex. The two power sources work together to make the car go. Because there are two ways to power the car, the gas engine can be smaller than the ones in gas-powered cars. It can also be turned off—even when the hybrid car is moving! In some hybrid cars, the gas engine turns off when the car is waiting at a stoplight or when it slows down.

The hybrid cars that are made today are different from many of the cars we are used to. They are made from lighter metals and plastics. They are shaped so that the wind does not push hard against them. They cannot always reach a high speed as quickly as a gas-powered car can. But, people still seem to want cars with hybrid engines. Why?

One big reason is that hybrid cars do not cause as much pollution. Because their gas engines are small and do not run constantly, the cars do not make as much *exhaust*, or gas fumes that go into the air. People who are worried about global warming say this is a good thing about the cars.

Make a prediction.

What do you think the author will write about next?

_____

Name_____ Date_____

Answer the following questions based on what you read on page 46. Then, finish reading the story at the bottom of the page.

1.–5. Write T for true and F for false.

1. _____ Hybrid cars pollute more than regular gas-powered cars.

2. _____ The word *hybrid* means "putting two things together."

3. _____ In some hybrid cars, the gas engine and the electric motor switch back and forth.

4. _____ A hybrid car does not need any gas.

5. _____ Hybrid cars cannot reach fast speeds as quickly as gas-powered cars can.

6. Which of the following words BEST completes this sentence?

   A hybrid car does not make as much _____ , or gas fumes.

   a. extreme
   b. exchange
   c. exhausted
   d. exhaust

7. The first part of the story tells about all of the following EXCEPT—

   a. how hybrid cars have different designs.
   b. why hybrid cars use both gas engines and electric motors.
   c. why hybrid cars don't pollute as much as gas-powered cars.
   d. how much hybrid cars cost.

A second reason that hybrid cars may be a good idea has to do with the cost of gas. Hybrid cars do not use as much gas as regular cars do. When gas costs rise, a hybrid car can save a lot of money. Many of these cars can go up to 400 miles on one tank of gas!

The earth's oil resources will be gone someday. Oil is used to make gas. As the amount of oil lessens, the cost of oil and gas will keep rising. That is why it is important to figure out how we can keep using our transportation without using as much oil. If scientists do this now, they may be able to solve the problem. Then, people will not need as much oil to run their cars and trucks. Are hybrid cars a good first step?

Conversion

400 miles = 643.74 kilometers

Next Page

What Is a Hybrid?

Answer the questions below.

8. Read the following sentence from the story and answer the question.

   As the amount of oil lessens, the cost of oil and gas will keep rising.

   Which of the following is an antonym for *lessens*?

   a. disappears
   b. grows
   c. expands
   d. b. and c.

9. Why would people who worry about global warming probably like hybrid cars?

   a. Hybrid cars don't pollute as much, and pollution may cause global warming.
   b. Hybrid cars cost less to run, which would help global warming.
   c. Hybrid cars are very expensive, so fewer people would drive if they couldn't afford a car.
   d. none of the above

10. In some hybrid cars,—

    a. the gas engines and electric motors have different jobs.
    b. the electric motors run the cars, and the gas engines are for emergencies.
    c. the gas goes into the batteries.
    d. the gas engines work all of the time.

11. One reason that hybrid cars might be a good idea is that they—

    a. pollute less.
    b. run faster.
    c. are heavier on the road.
    d. b. and c.

12. What can you infer about why hybrid cars could help to solve oil problems?

    a. If there is less oil, people will need cars that don't use as much gas.
    b. If there are only hybrid cars, people will need more oil, not less.
    c. Hybrid cars use electricity and gas, so they use less gas than regular cars.
    d. a. and c.

13. Would you like to have a hybrid car? Why or why not? Write your answer in complete sentences.

    _____

    _____

    _____

    _____

    _____

STOP

Cars of the Future

Will **cars of the future** run on gas? Many people do not think so. They think that new cars will be invented. These new cars would use different things for fuel. The new fuel would be better for the environment. It would be cheaper than gas. It would help cars run longer for less money.

People do not agree about what the new fuel should be. Some people say electricity would be a good fuel. We already put electric motors that run on batteries into machines that used to run on gas. One example is the lawn mower. We also put electric motors in hybrid cars. Could cars run only on batteries?

One problem is what might happen when the batteries run low. When a car runs out of gas, the driver buys more. But, it takes time to charge a battery. Many people do not want to sit and wait for batteries to charge before they can continue driving.

Fuel cells are another idea for fueling cars. Like batteries, fuel cells create energy with a chemical reaction. Unlike batteries, fuel cells don't need to be recharged. These cells run on liquid hydrogen, which can be changed into a gas. Some fuel-cell cars have even been tested. The fuel-cell car cannot go as fast as a gas car. It has to be made of lighter metals. But, it can drive about 120 miles before it needs more fuel. And, it does not pollute the air at all.

What are the drawbacks of fuel-cell cars? One problem is the cost. Building these cars costs a lot of money. Another problem is that people would have to change all of the gas stations in the world! Right now, if you drove a fuel-cell car, you would have no place to buy hydrogen when it runs out. Some people say that figuring out where to get the hydrogen for the cars is hard, too.

Make a prediction.

What do you think the author will write about next?

_____

Conversions

120 miles = 193.12 kilometers

Answer the following questions based on what you read on page 49. Then, finish reading the story at the bottom of the page.

1. A fuel cell uses _____,

   which can be turned into a gas.

2. Fuel cells do not _____

   the air.

3. If you drove a fuel-cell car right now,

   you would have nowhere to get more

   _____ .

4. Cars that run on electricity would need

   _____ to run.

5. Cars that do not use gas would cost

   _____ to run.

Other people say that getting hydrogen is not a problem at all. Instead of going to a station to buy it, people can make hydrogen at home using electricity and water. But, that is a very slow process. Are there other ways to make hydrogen for these cars of the future?

Could cars of the future run on sunflowers? Some scientists in England think so. They are studying a way of making hydrogen from sunflower oil. Their idea is to put the sunflower oil into a tank in the car. Then, a special part of the engine would pull the hydrogen out of the oil. The problem with this idea? The scientists are having trouble making the engine small enough to fit into a car. Right now, the sunflower-oil engine is 3,000 times bigger than a regular gas engine!

What about the sun? The sun has a huge amount of power. Could it be used to power fuel cells? Some scientists are trying this idea. They say that hydrogen could be made from the sun's ultraviolet rays. Ultraviolet rays are present even on cloudy days. So, this idea could work. But, hydrogen would have to be stored somehow for driving at night. Scientists are still working on this and many other ideas for the cars of the future.

Next Page

Name _____ Date _____

Cars of the Future

Answer the questions below.

6. Read the following sentences from the story and answer the question.

   Then, a special part of the engine would pull the hydrogen out of the oil. The problem with this idea?

   What kind of phrase is *The problem with this idea*?

   a. a declarative sentence
   b. a fragment
   c. an exclamation
   d. a prepositional phrase

7. The story discusses all of the following EXCEPT—

   a. electric cars.
   b. cars that run on sunflower oil.
   c. cars powered by the sun.
   d. cars that run on compost.

8. Read the following sentence from the story and answer the question.

   The new fuel would be better for the environment.

   What is a word or phrase that could be used to replace *the environment* in this sentence?

   a. our planet
   b. our universe
   c. Earth
   d. a. and c.

9. What is the biggest problem with the sunflower-oil car?

   a. There are not enough sunflowers to run it.
   b. The engine doesn't work.
   c. The engine is too big.
   d. The flowers are too small.

10. Which of the following is the MOST difficult problem for cars powered by the sun?

    a. They won't work on cloudy days.
    b. They may not work on sunny days.
    c. They may not work at night.
    d. They don't run fast enough.

11.–13. Write T for true and F for false.

11. _____ Ultraviolet rays are present on both sunny days and cloudy days.

12. _____ Liquid hydrogen must be changed into a gas to work in a fuel cell.

13. _____ People can make liquid hydrogen at home, but it takes a long time.

STOP

A Wild Ride

A ride on a **roller coaster** is exciting! A roller coaster plunges down hills. It races around corners. The feeling can make your stomach jump and your head spin. Have you ever wondered how it all works?

A roller coaster is an amazing machine. It seems like it would need a lot of help to go around all of those twists and turns. But, roller coasters are mostly run by nature!

How is this possible? A machine pulls the roller coaster cars up the first hill. On simple roller coasters, the machine is like a towrope. Chains help pull the cars up this hill, called the *lift hill*. Then, the chains are released. The roller coaster is pulled down the hill by gravity. When it heads up the next hill, gravity slows the tail end of the roller coaster. That is why it seems to slow down and speed up throughout the ride.

Many roller coasters are built with hills that get smaller and smaller. The biggest hill is almost always the lift hill. This makes sure there is plenty of energy for the rest of the ride! And, as the roller coaster goes over the smaller hills, it starts to slow. Finally, it coasts to a stop.

There are two basic kinds of roller coasters. The older kind is made of wood. It has tracks that look like railroad tracks. Part of the fun of wooden roller coasters is the way the tracks rattle. The cars sway from side to side. But, wood is hard to bend. That means it is hard to make a wooden roller coaster with lots of twists and turns. Most of the excitement comes from lots of hills.

Make a prediction.

What do you think the author will write about next?

Next Page ➡

Answer the following questions based on what you read on page 52. Then, finish reading the story at the bottom of the page.

1. Why does the story say that roller coasters are run by nature?

    a. Roller coasters are natural objects.
    b. Roller coasters depend on gravity.
    c. Roller coasters are exciting.
    d. Roller coasters are built using natural objects.

2. The tracks on a wooden roller coaster are built like—

    a. highway exits.
    b. lift hills.
    c. train tracks.
    d. racetracks.

3. Read the following sentences from the story and answer the question.

    And, as the roller coaster goes over the smaller hills, it starts to slow. Finally, it coasts to a stop.

    What does *coasts* mean as it is used in the second sentence?

    a. places where the land meets the sea
    b. slowly stopping without brakes
    c. to travel past the side of something
    d. to race past something

The second kind of roller coaster is made of steel. Some of these roller coasters run on tracks, like a train. Others run on rails, like a subway. Steel tracks are easier to bend. So, steel roller coasters have more turns. Sometimes, the cars even go upside down! The tracks are made in huge pieces. They look like pieces of a skyscraper. The tracks are put together using few joints in the steel. This makes the ride smooth and fast. Two sets of wheels keep the cars from going off the tracks.

You can find roller coasters at *amusement parks*, or places with many rides and other fun things to do. At many parks, roller coasters are the most popular rides. With thrilling twists, turns, and plunges, it is no wonder that people love roller coasters!

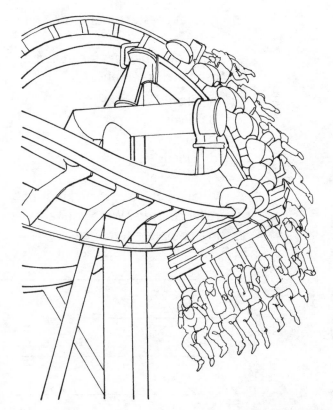

Next Page

A Wild Ride

Answer the questions below.

4. Why does the lift hill have to be the biggest hill on the ride?

    a. Going down the big hill makes the energy for the rest of the ride.
    b. Wood is hard to bend to make the tracks.
    c. Roller coasters need to be pulled and pushed by a lift machine.
    d. Roller coasters are made of steel.

5. Read the following sentence from the story and answer the question.

    A roller coaster plunges down hills.

    What does *plunges* mean as it is used in this sentence?

    a. skates
    b. dives
    c. jumps
    d. crawls

6. What are the two main kinds of roller coasters? Write your answer in a complete sentence.

    _____

    _____

    _____

    _____

7. What is ONE main feature of a steel roller coaster?

    a. It has more hills.
    b. It has higher hills.
    c. It has no brakes.
    d. It has more twists and turns.

8. Read the following sentence from the story and answer the question.

    The tracks are put together using few joints in the steel.

    What is another word for *joints*?

    a. seams
    b. tracks
    c. corners
    d. twists

9. Which type of roller coaster do you think you would like better? Why? Write your answer in complete sentences.

    _____

    _____

    _____

    _____

STOP

At Home in Space

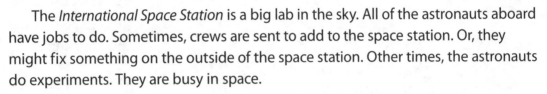

Space stations have been in space since 1973. That was the year that the United States launched *Skylab*. In 1998, the first section of the *International Space Station* was launched. Today, the station is run by several different countries working together. What is life like aboard this fascinating machine?

The *International Space Station* is a big lab in the sky. All of the astronauts aboard have jobs to do. Sometimes, crews are sent to add to the space station. Or, they might fix something on the outside of the space station. Other times, the astronauts do experiments. They are busy in space.

When astronauts have to work outside the space station, they can't just walk out the door! The astronauts have to put on very heavy space suits. They each weigh 250 pounds. If you wore such a heavy suit on Earth, you would find it hard to move! But, in space, things are weightless. The suit does not feel heavy in space. It helps an astronaut breathe and provides safety from the cold or heat outside the space station. The suit is linked to the station with a *tether*, or safety rope. If the rope weren't there, the astronaut would float into space.

Inside the space station, astronauts work in the labs. They also exercise. It is very important for the astronauts to stay fit. They work out for two hours every day that they are in space. The space station has a stationary bike and a treadmill. These help keep the astronauts healthy. It helps them get ready for the hard jobs that they do in the space station.

Living in a weightless home can be hard. On Earth, when you put something down, it stays there. That's not true in a space station! This changes how astronauts do everyday things. They have to learn how to be careful while they are working, resting, and even sleeping.

Conversion
250 pounds = 113.4 kilograms

Next Page

At Home in Space

Answer the following questions based on what you read on page 55. Then, finish reading the story on the next page.

1. The first part of the story is MOSTLY about—
   a. working aboard a space station.
   b. the space program in the United States.
   c. the history of space stations.
   d. none of the above

2. How much does a space suit weigh on Earth?
   a. nothing
   b. 150 pounds
   c. 200 pounds
   d. 250 pounds

3. What was *Skylab*?
   a. the first space station
   b. a space station launched in 1973
   c. a space station made by Russian scientists
   d. a. and b.

4. What is the MAIN reason that an astronaut has to wear a space suit outside a space station?
   a. to carry tools
   b. to float into space
   c. to stay in shape
   d. to breathe

Conversions

150 pounds = 68.04 kilograms
200 pounds = 90.72 kilograms
250 pounds = 113.4 kilograms

5. According to the story, what are two things that an astronaut might do during a day in a space station?
   a. exercise and talk on the telephone
   b. work outside and travel to another planet
   c. work in a lab and exercise
   d. take a day off and snack

6. Read the following sentence from the story and answer the question.

   They work out for two hours every day that they are in space.

   According to the story, why is this true?
   a. Astronauts like to use the treadmill.
   b. Astronauts need to stay healthy.
   c. Astronauts have to be ready to do hard work.
   d. b. and c.

7. What do you think the author will write about next? Write your answer in a complete sentence.

   _____

   _____

   _____

Next Page

**Finish reading "At Home in Space" below.
Then, answer the questions on page 58.**

Life without gravity inside a space station changes everything. The astronauts cannot take showers. Water would just float into the air! They have to take baths with sponges to wash themselves. They use dry shampoo to clean their hair.

Another job that is hard is cleaning. On Earth, dust falls down. It lands on floors and the tops of things. In space, dust goes everywhere. Astronauts spend time wiping dust off the walls and ceilings of their rooms. They also clean the fans so that dust doesn't stop the air system from working.

Cooking is not very hard in space. That is because all of the cooking is done before the astronauts leave Earth. The *International Space Station* has an oven to heat the cooked food. When the first astronauts went into space, they ate food that was turned into powder or dried. Today, astronauts can take fresh food into space. They have juice, vegetables, and fruit. They eat pasta and seafood. Eating can be tricky, though. Food is held inside special dishes with tops so that it doesn't fly off the plates! Juice and water are held in bottles or bags. Astronauts never have to wash the dishes. They just throw the dishes in the trash can when they are done. This saves water.

One of the strangest parts of life in a space station is sleeping. On Earth, gravity keeps you in your bed. In a space station, each astronaut has a bedroom like a big closet. They have sleeping bags. These bags snap onto the wall, the floor, or even the ceiling. The bags have to be attached so that astronauts don't float away at bedtime. Astronauts are zipped into the bags. Then, they strap down their heads! In space, a person's head doesn't just stay on the pillow. There are also straps shaped like loops for the astronauts' hands to keep their arms close to their bodies. Astronauts need lots of rest so that they are ready for the next day. They have to run a huge machine as it orbits Earth!

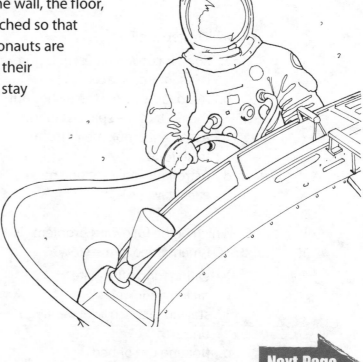

Next Page

Name_____ Date_____

At Home in Space

Answer the questions below.

8. The author writes about the food that astronauts eat. Look at the chain of events below and answer the question.

Astronauts heat food in an oven.

↓

Lids keep food from floating off the plates.

↓

Astronauts finish the meal.

↓

The dishes are thrown away to save water.

Which step is missing?

a. Food is cooked on Earth before it is sent into space.
b. Astronauts throw the dishes out the door of the space station.
c. Astronauts cook meals from fresh food.
d. Astronauts only eat one meal each day.

9. Which of the following problems is NOT mentioned in the story?

a. eating food off a plate
b. taking a shower
c. staying in touch with family on Earth
d. floating out of bed

10. Read the following sentence from the story and answer the question.

They have to run a huge machine as it orbits Earth!

What is a synonym for *orbits*?

a. races
b. plunges
c. travels
d. circles

11. Why do astronauts have to strap down their heads when they sleep?

a. Gravity does not keep their heads on the pillows like it does on Earth.
b. The head straps keep their heads safe if there is a crash.
c. The pillows on a space station are hard and small.
d. In space, their heads weigh so much that it is dangerous.

12. What makes cleaning hard inside a space station?

a. Dust only gets on the floors.
b. Dust can go in any direction.
c. Dust can make the astronauts sneeze when they are in their space suits.
d. There is more dust in space.

The Most Fascinating Machine

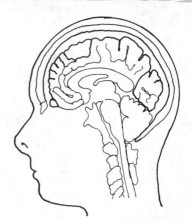

What is the most complicated "machine" in the world? It is the **human brain**! Your brain controls everything about you. It keeps your heart beating. It tells you how to move your body. It makes sure your body is the right temperature. It helps you see, feel, taste, hear, and smell. Your brain stores all of your memories. It is the place where all of your thoughts and ideas begin.

The brain is actually not very big. This is surprising since it does so much. But, this critical *organ*, or body part, only weighs about three pounds. It makes up less than two percent of your whole body. Without it, nothing in your body would work.

How does the brain do all of its work? It sends messages to every part of the body. To do this, it uses *neurons*, or nerve cells. Neurons use a linking method, called *synapses*, to send information from the brain to other parts of the body. Synapses are the tiny spaces between the neurons. There are over 100 billion neurons in your brain. They send commands across one quadrillion synapses. These commands are like electrical sparks, and they make every part of your body work!

Even when you are asleep, your brain is working. It makes you dream. It checks the temperature of your body. It tells your muscles if your body is too hot or too cold. Then, it sends messages that tell your body to move around in your bed. If you push your blanket away while you are asleep, it is because your brain told you to do it!

Different parts of the brain take care of different parts of the body. The upper part of your brain, shaped like a bike helmet, takes care of memory and feelings. It takes message from all of your senses. The lower part of your brain takes care of your body movements. The brain stem, in the lower back of the brain, is in charge of things like your heart, blood movement, and hunger.

What happens if something hurts a person's brain?

Conversion

3 pounds = 1.36 kilograms

Next Page

The Most Fascinating Machine

Answer the following questions based on what you read on page 59. Then, finish reading the story on the next page.

1. Synapses are like—

    a. safety ropes.
    b. nerves.
    c. tiny gaps between wires.
    d. big holes in the road.

2. Why does the author say it is surprising that the brain only weighs three pounds?

    a. It is surprising because that's very heavy.
    b. It is surprising because the brain does so much to be so small.
    c. It is surprising that the brain doesn't weigh less.
    d. It is surprising that the brain needs so much room.

3. What is a *neuron*?

    a. a connection between one cell and another
    b. a nerve cell
    c. a linking system
    d. a memory cell

4. What does your brain control?

    a. the beating of your heart
    b. your body temperature
    c. the movement of your body
    d. all of the above

5.–9. Write T for true or F for false.

5. _____ Your dreams are created by your brain.

6. _____ The brain stem controls your thoughts and feelings.

7. _____ The upper part of the brain is shaped like a ball.

8. _____ Neurons are linked by synapses.

9. _____ The lower part of your brain controls body movements.

10. What do you think the author will write about next? Write your answer in a complete sentence.

    _____

    _____

    _____

    _____

    _____

    _____

Next Page →

Finish reading "The Most Fascinating Machine" below. Then, answer the questions on page 62.

It depends on which part gets hurt. Sometimes, an injury to the brain will stop a person from being able to move. Other times, it will make the person lose memory. It also might make it hard for the person to speak. It is important to take care of the brain. When a brain cell is hurt, it cannot be fixed again. And, without the cells of this fascinating machine, we could never invent any other fascinating machines!

So, how can you take care of your brain? There are simple things you can do to make sure that your brain stays healthy. Drugs and alcohol can kill brain cells, so staying away from drugs and alcohol is important. Always wear a helmet when you ride your bike to help keep your head—and your brain—safe.

Sleep is very important to your brain. That's why you will sleep for one-third of your lifetime. By the time you are 80 years old, you will have spent more than 26 years of your life asleep! Scientists are not exactly sure why the brain needs sleep. But, they know that without sleep, the brain cannot work correctly.

In addition to sleep, your brain also gets energy from what you eat. Do you think "brain food" really exists? Scientists say that some foods are better for the brain than others. The fats found in fish and vegetable oils help renew your brain. Eggs may help you remember more. Dark green vegetables can make you think better and be in a better mood.

Are there other ways to take care of your brain? Here's one amazing way: learn new things! The brain stays healthy when you learn. Playing word games, reading about science or history, or learning to play music are just a few ways that you can "feed" your brain with new ideas. Exercising and playing games also helps your brain focus. If you keep learning and moving throughout your life, your brain will be quicker and healthier.

Next Page ➤

The Most Fascinating Machine

Answer the questions below.

11. Read the following sentence from the story and answer the question.

    The fats found in fish and vegetable oils help renew your brain.

    What is a synonym for *renew*?

    a. reshape
    b. recapture
    c. recent
    d. refresh

12. What can happen when the brain is hurt?

    a. A person might have trouble talking.
    b. A person might lose her memory.
    c. A person might not be able to walk or move.
    d. all of the above

13. Which part of the brain is shaped like a bike helmet?

    a. the upper part of the brain
    b. the brain stem
    c. the lower part of the brain
    d. a neuron

14. Based on what the story says about keeping brains healthy, what can you infer might help your brain?

    a. doing a crossword puzzle
    b. watching an old show on TV
    c. chewing gum
    d. none of the above

15. The story talks about all of these things EXCEPT—

    a. how food can affect your brain.
    b. what happens when brain cells get hurt.
    c. how animal brains are different from human brains.
    d. how to feed your brain with new ideas.

16. According to the story, what is the reason that sleep is important for the brain?

    a. The story says that sleep helps to fix hurt brain cells.
    b. The story says that sleep is important to the brain because of dreams.
    c. The story says that we don't know why sleep is important to the brain.
    d. all of the above

17. Explain how you plan to keep your brain healthy. Write your answer in complete sentences.

    _____

    _____

    _____

    _____

Answer Key

Page 6
1. d. 2. a.
3. ax, splits things apart, drives into something
4. a.
5. energy, movement, clock
6. d.
7. Answers will vary.

Page 8
1. b. 2. a. 3. b.
4. An abacus is a counting board with beads on it.
5. d.
6. Answers will vary.

Page 10
1. a.
2. A crane uses a pulley and a wheel and axle.
3. F 4. T 5. F
6. T 7. d. 8. d.
9. Answers will vary.

Page 12
1. c. 2. a. 3. d.
4. planes
5. weather
6. the sun
7. signals
8. a.
9. Answers will vary.

Page 14
1. A receiver is a small object that can pick up signals from satellites.
2. c. 3. F 4. T 5. T
6. F 7. T 8. a.
9. a. the armed forces
   b. computers
   c. signals
10. Answers will vary.

Page 16
1. b. 2. c. 3. c.
4. c. 5. d. 6. a.
7. Answers will vary.

Page 18
1. c. 2. b.
3. b. 4. d.
5. Answers will vary.

Page 20
1. e. 2. d. 3. b. 4. c.
5. a. 6. c. 7. c.
8. a. tourists
   b. slope (or beach)
   c. ambulance
9. a. is not
   b. 40
   c. World War II
   d. wheels

Page 22
1. Japan
2. 200; 300
3. Europe
4. plane
5. 1959
6. T 7. F 8. T
9. T 10. d.
11. Answers will vary.

Page 24
1. b. 2. a. 3. d.
4. d. 5. c.
6. Answers will vary.

Page 26
1. a. 2. d. 3. b. 4. F
5. T 6. T 7. a.
8. Answers will vary but may include: There's no paper trail to verify the votes or check that the computers are working properly.

Page 28
1. b. 2. d. 3. a. 4. a.
5. the *White Knight*
6. space station
7. a special type of gas
8. Answers will vary.

Page 30
1. c. 2. a. 3. b.
4. Spy planes can fly closer to the ground and take close-up pictures.
5. Answers will vary but may include:
   a. can be carried in a backpack
   b. only weighs three pounds
   c. takes pictures that are instantly sent to the computer
6. d.
7. Answers will vary.

Page 31
the third machine

Page 32
1. c. 2. d.
3. Answers will vary but may include: Argo is like a giant underwater sled that is equipped with sonar and cameras.
4. c.

Page 33
5. d. 6. b. 7. a.
8. c. 9. d.
10. Answers will vary but may include:
   a. built for deep sea diving
   b. can land on the sea floor
   c. holds three people

Page 34
robots of the future

Page 35
1. b.   2. c.   3. d.

Page 36
4. F   5. T   6. T
7. T   8. d.   9. d.
10. Answers will vary but
    may include:
    a. talk and listen
    b. write
    c. be able to learn
11. Answers will vary.

Page 37
future help for eyes

Page 38
1. light
2. Netherlands
3. pupil
4. curves
5. c.   6. c.

Page 39
7. opinion
8. b.   9. a.   10. b.   11. c.

Page 40
what happens when a
computer gets "sick"

Page 41
1. Answers will vary but may
   include:
   a. gives memory to programs
   b. sorts all of the jobs
   c. acts like a traffic officer
2. d.   3. d.

Page 42
4. software, program,
   operating system
5. a.   6. c.   7. d.   8. d.
9. Answers will vary but may
   include: No, a TV doesn't
   need an operating system
   because it only does one job,
   like a coffee maker.

Page 43
Mars rovers' other jobs

Page 44
1. b.   2. a.   3. b.
4. Answers will vary but may
   include: A Mars rover is a
   robot that explores Mars and
   sends data to Earth.

Page 45
5. b.   6. d.   7. a.
8. c.   9. d.
10. Answers will vary but may
    include: Space shuttles can't
    land on Mars to pick up the
    rovers. It would be too
    expensive to try to get them.

Page 46
other reasons people want
hybrid cars

Page 47
1. F   2. T   3. T   4. F
5. T   6. d.   7. d.

Page 48
8. d.   9. a.   10. a.
11. a.   12. d.
13. Answers will vary.

Page 49
ways to get hydrogen
for fuel cells

Page 50
1. liquid hydrogen
2. pollute
3. hydrogen (or fuel)
4. batteries
5. less

Page 51
6. b.   7. d.   8. d.   9. c.
10. c.   11. T   12. T   13. T

Page 52
the second type of
roller coaster

Page 53
1. b.   2. c.   3. b.

Page 54
4. a.   5. b.
6. The two main kinds of roller
   coasters have wooden tracks
   and steel tracks.
7. d.   8. a.
9. Answers will vary.

Page 56
1. a.   2. d.   3. d.
4. d.   5. c.   6. d.
7. The author will describe
   living in a weightless home.

Page 58
8. a.   9. c.   10. d.
11. a.   12. b.

Page 60
1. c.   2. b.   3. b.   4. d.
5. T   6. F   7. F   8. T
9. T
10. The story will tell about
    what happens when the
    brain is injured.

Page 62
11. d.   12. d.   13. a.
14. a.   15. c.   16. c.
17. Answers will vary.